This Book Belongs to

_____

SUPPLIERS INFO:

Name _____ Shop _____ Location _____
Phone _____ Email _____ _____
Tele _____ Web _____ _____

Name _____ Shop _____ Location _____
Phone _____ Email _____ _____
Tele _____ Web _____ _____

Name _____ Shop _____ Location _____
Phone _____ Email _____ _____
Tele _____ Web _____ _____

Name _____ Shop _____ Location _____
Phone _____ Email _____ _____
Tele _____ Web _____ _____

Name _____ Shop _____ Location _____
Phone _____ Email _____ _____
Tele _____ Web _____ _____

Name _____ Shop _____ Location _____
Phone _____ Email _____ _____
Tele _____ Web _____ _____

Name _____ Shop _____ Location _____
Phone _____ Email _____ _____
Tele _____ Web _____ _____

Name _____ Shop _____ Location _____
Phone _____ Email _____ _____
Tele _____ Web _____ _____

Name _____ Shop _____ Location _____
Phone _____ Email _____ _____
Tele _____ Web _____ _____

Name _____ Shop _____ Location _____
Phone _____ Email _____ _____
Tele _____ Web _____ _____

SUPPLIERS INFO:

Name _____ Shop _____ Location _____
Phone _____ Email _____ _____
Tele _____ Web _____ _____

Name _____ Shop _____ Location _____
Phone _____ Email _____ _____
Tele _____ Web _____ _____

Name _____ Shop _____ Location _____
Phone _____ Email _____ _____
Tele _____ Web _____ _____

Name _____ Shop _____ Location _____
Phone _____ Email _____ _____
Tele _____ Web _____ _____

Name _____ Shop _____ Location _____
Phone _____ Email _____ _____
Tele _____ Web _____ _____

Name _____ Shop _____ Location _____
Phone _____ Email _____ _____
Tele _____ Web _____ _____

Name _____ Shop _____ Location _____
Phone _____ Email _____ _____
Tele _____ Web _____ _____

Name _____ Shop _____ Location _____
Phone _____ Email _____ _____
Tele _____ Web _____ _____

Name _____ Shop _____ Location _____
Phone _____ Email _____ _____
Tele _____ Web _____ _____

Name _____ Shop _____ Location _____
Phone _____ Email _____ _____
Tele _____ Web _____ _____

GARDEN LAYOUT

GARDEN LAYOUT

Seasonal To Do List

Spring

- [ ] _____
- [ ] _____
- [ ] _____
- [ ] _____
- [ ] _____
- [ ] _____
- [ ] _____
- [ ] _____
- [ ] _____
- [ ] _____

Summer

- [ ] _____
- [ ] _____
- [ ] _____
- [ ] _____
- [ ] _____
- [ ] _____
- [ ] _____
- [ ] _____
- [ ] _____
- [ ] _____

Fall

- [ ] _____
- [ ] _____
- [ ] _____
- [ ] _____
- [ ] _____
- [ ] _____
- [ ] _____
- [ ] _____
- [ ] _____

Winter

- [ ] _____
- [ ] _____
- [ ] _____
- [ ] _____
- [ ] _____
- [ ] _____
- [ ] _____
- [ ] _____
- [ ] _____

YEAR AT GLANCE

JANUARY	FEBRUARY	MARCH

APRIL	MAY	JUNE

JULY	AUGUST	SEPTEMBER

OCTOBER	NOVEMBER	DECEMBER

JANUARY CALENDAR

Monday	Tuesday	Wednesday	Thursday	Friday	Saturday	Sunday

TO DO LIST

- [ ] _____
- [ ] _____
- [ ] _____
- [ ] _____
- [ ] _____
- [ ] _____
- [ ] _____
- [ ] _____
- [ ] _____
- [ ] _____
- [ ] _____
- [ ] _____
- [ ] _____
- [ ] _____
- [ ] _____
- [ ] _____
- [ ] _____

PRIORITIES

_____
_____
_____
_____
_____
_____

SOW / TRANSPLANT

_____   _____
_____   _____
_____   _____
_____   _____
_____   _____
_____   _____
_____   _____
_____   _____
_____   _____
_____   _____
_____   _____
_____   _____
_____   _____
_____   _____
_____   _____
_____   _____
_____   _____

NOTES

_____
_____
_____
_____
_____

SHOPPING LIST

NOTES

FEBRUARY CALENDAR

Monday	Tuesday	Wednesday	Thursday	Friday	Saturday	Sunday

Monday	Tuesday	Wednesday	Thursday	Friday	Saturday	Sunday

TO DO LIST

- [ ]
- [ ]
- [ ]
- [ ]
- [ ]
- [ ]
- [ ]
- [ ]
- [ ]
- [ ]
- [ ]
- [ ]
- [ ]
- [ ]
- [ ]
- [ ]
- [ ]
- [ ]

PRIORITIES

SOW / TRANSPLANT

NOTES

SHOPPING LIST

NOTES

MARCH CALENDAR

Monday	Tuesday	Wednesday	Thursday	Friday	Saturday	Sunday

TO DO LIST

- [ ]
- [ ]
- [ ]
- [ ]
- [ ]
- [ ]
- [ ]
- [ ]
- [ ]
- [ ]
- [ ]
- [ ]
- [ ]
- [ ]
- [ ]
- [ ]
- [ ]

PRIORITIES

SOW / TRANSPLANT

_____

_____

_____

_____

_____

_____

_____

_____

_____

_____

_____

_____

_____

_____

_____

_____

_____

_____

NOTES

_____

_____

_____

_____

_____

_____

SHOPPING LIST

_____   _____
_____   _____
_____   _____
_____   _____
_____   _____
_____   _____
_____   _____
_____   _____
_____   _____
_____   _____

NOTES

_____
_____
_____
_____
_____
_____
_____
_____
_____
_____

APRIL CALENDAR

Monday	Tuesday	Wednesday	Thursday	Friday	Saturday	Sunday

TO DO LIST

- [ ]
- [ ]
- [ ]
- [ ]
- [ ]
- [ ]
- [ ]
- [ ]
- [ ]
- [ ]
- [ ]
- [ ]
- [ ]
- [ ]
- [ ]
- [ ]
- [ ]
- [ ]

PRIORITIES

SOW / TRANSPLANT

_____   _____
_____   _____
_____   _____
_____   _____
_____   _____
_____   _____
_____   _____
_____   _____
_____   _____
_____   _____
_____   _____
_____   _____
_____   _____
_____   _____
_____   _____
_____   _____
_____   _____

NOTES

_____
_____
_____
_____
_____

SHOPPING LIST

NOTES

MAY CALENDAR

Monday	Tuesday	Wednesday	Thursday	Friday	Saturday	Sunday

TO DO LIST

- ☐
- ☐
- ☐
- ☐
- ☐
- ☐
- ☐
- ☐
- ☐
- ☐
- ☐
- ☐
- ☐
- ☐
- ☐
- ☐
- ☐
- ☐

PRIORITIES

SOW / TRANSPLANT

NOTES

SHOPPING LIST

_____   _____
_____   _____
_____   _____
_____   _____
_____   _____
_____   _____
_____   _____
_____   _____
_____   _____
_____   _____
_____   _____

NOTES

_____
_____
_____
_____
_____
_____
_____
_____
_____
_____
_____

JUNE CALENDAR

Monday	Tuesday	Wednesday	Thursday	Friday	Saturday	Sunday

TO DO LIST

- [ ]
- [ ]
- [ ]
- [ ]
- [ ]
- [ ]
- [ ]
- [ ]
- [ ]
- [ ]
- [ ]
- [ ]
- [ ]
- [ ]
- [ ]
- [ ]
- [ ]
- [ ]

PRIORITIES

SOW / TRANSPLANT

_____   _____

_____   _____

_____   _____

_____   _____

_____   _____

_____   _____

_____   _____

_____   _____

_____   _____

_____   _____

_____   _____

_____   _____

_____   _____

NOTES

_____

_____

_____

_____

_____

SHOPPING LIST

NOTES

JULY CALENDAR

Monday	Tuesday	Wednesday	Thursday	Friday	Saturday	Sunday

TO DO LIST

- [ ]
- [ ]
- [ ]
- [ ]
- [ ]
- [ ]
- [ ]
- [ ]
- [ ]
- [ ]
- [ ]
- [ ]
- [ ]
- [ ]
- [ ]
- [ ]
- [ ]
- [ ]

PRIORITIES

SOW / TRANSPLANT

NOTES

SHOPPING LIST

NOTES

AUGUST CALENDAR

Monday	Tuesday	Wednesday	Thursday	Friday	Saturday	Sunday

TO DO LIST

- [ ]
- [ ]
- [ ]
- [ ]
- [ ]
- [ ]
- [ ]
- [ ]
- [ ]
- [ ]
- [ ]
- [ ]
- [ ]
- [ ]
- [ ]
- [ ]
- [ ]

PRIORITIES

SOW / TRANSPLANT

_____

_____

_____

_____

_____

_____

_____

_____

_____

_____

_____

_____

_____

_____

_____

_____

_____

NOTES

_____

_____

_____

_____

_____

_____

SHOPPING LIST

NOTES

SEPTEMBER CALENDAR

Monday	Tuesday	Wednesday	Thursday	Friday	Saturday	Sunday

TO DO LIST

- [ ]
- [ ]
- [ ]
- [ ]
- [ ]
- [ ]
- [ ]
- [ ]
- [ ]
- [ ]
- [ ]
- [ ]
- [ ]
- [ ]
- [ ]
- [ ]
- [ ]
- [ ]
- [ ]

PRIORITIES

SOW / TRANSPLANT

_____

_____

_____

_____

_____

_____

_____

_____

_____

_____

_____

_____

_____

_____

_____

_____

NOTES

_____

_____

_____

_____

_____

SHOPPING LIST

NOTES

OCTOBER CALENDAR

Monday	Tuesday	Wednesday	Thursday	Friday	Saturday	Sunday

TO DO LIST

- [ ]
- [ ]
- [ ]
- [ ]
- [ ]
- [ ]
- [ ]
- [ ]
- [ ]
- [ ]
- [ ]
- [ ]
- [ ]
- [ ]
- [ ]
- [ ]
- [ ]

PRIORITIES

SOW / TRANSPLANT

_____

_____

_____

_____

_____

_____

_____

_____

_____

_____

_____

_____

_____

_____

_____

_____

_____

_____

NOTES

_____

_____

_____

_____

_____

_____

SHOPPING LIST

NOTES

NOVEMBER CALENDAR

Monday	Tuesday	Wednesday	Thursday	Friday	Saturday	Sunday

TO DO LIST

- [ ] _____
- [ ] _____
- [ ] _____
- [ ] _____
- [ ] _____
- [ ] _____
- [ ] _____
- [ ] _____
- [ ] _____
- [ ] _____
- [ ] _____
- [ ] _____
- [ ] _____
- [ ] _____
- [ ] _____
- [ ] _____
- [ ] _____
- [ ] _____

PRIORITIES

_____

_____

_____

_____

_____

SOW / TRANSPLANT

NOTES

SHOPPING LIST

_____   _____
_____   _____
_____   _____
_____   _____
_____   _____
_____   _____
_____   _____
_____   _____
_____   _____
_____   _____
_____   _____
_____   _____

NOTES

_____
_____
_____
_____
_____
_____
_____
_____
_____
_____
_____
_____

DECEMBER CALENDAR

Monday	Tuesday	Wednesday	Thursday	Friday	Saturday	Sunday

TO DO LIST

- [ ] _____
- [ ] _____
- [ ] _____
- [ ] _____
- [ ] _____
- [ ] _____
- [ ] _____
- [ ] _____
- [ ] _____
- [ ] _____
- [ ] _____
- [ ] _____
- [ ] _____
- [ ] _____
- [ ] _____
- [ ] _____

PRIORITIES

_____
_____
_____
_____
_____

SOW / TRANSPLANT

_____ | _____
_____ | _____
_____ | _____
_____ | _____
_____ | _____
_____ | _____
_____ | _____
_____ | _____
_____ | _____
_____ | _____
_____ | _____
_____ | _____
_____ | _____
_____ | _____
_____ | _____
_____ | _____

NOTES

_____
_____
_____
_____
_____

SHOPPING LIST

NOTES

Plant Name:	Purchased at:
Date Planted:	Price:

Sunlight: ☼ ☼ ●

Water: 💧 💧💧 💧💧💧

○ Seed
○ Transplant

Plant Type
○ Vegetable ○ Ornamental
○ Fruit ○ Herb

Life Cycle: ○ Annual   ○ Biennial   ○ Perennial

SOWN FROM SEED	STARTED TRANSPLANT
Supplier:	Supplier:
Cost:	Cost:
Date Sown:	Date Planted:
Date Germinated:	Date Bloomed:
Date Planted Out:	**RATE IT:** ☆ ☆ ☆ ☆ ☆
Date Bloomed:	

Date	Event

Outcome	Uses

Notes

Plant Name:	Purchased at:
Date Planted:	Price:

Sunlight: ☼ ☼ ●

Water: 🌢 🌢🌢 🌢🌢🌢

○ Seed
○ Transplant

Plant Type
○ Vegetable   ○ Ornamental
○ Fruit   ○ Herb

Life Cycle: ○ Annual   ○ Biennial   ○ Perennial

SOWN FROM SEED	STARTED TRANSPLANT
Supplier:	Supplier:
Cost:	Cost:
Date Sown:	Date Planted:
Date Germinated:	Date Bloomed:
Date Planted Out:	**RATE IT:** ☆☆☆☆☆
Date Bloomed:	

Date	Event

Outcome	Uses

Notes

Plant Name:	Purchased at:
Date Planted:	Price:

Sunlight: ☼ ☼ ●

Water: 🌢 🌢🌢 🌢🌢🌢

○ Seed
○ Transplant

Plant Type
○ Vegetable   ○ Ornamental
○ Fruit   ○ Herb

Life Cycle: ○ Annual   ○ Biennial   ○ Perennial

SOWN FROM SEED	STARTED TRANSPLANT
Supplier:	Supplier:
Cost:	Cost:
Date Sown:	Date Planted:
Date Germinated:	Date Bloomed:
Date Planted Out	**RATE IT:** ☆ ☆ ☆ ☆ ☆
Date Bloomed:	

Date	Event

Outcome	Uses

Notes

Plant Name:	Purchased at:
Date Planted:	Price:

Sunlight: ☼ ☼ ●

Water: 🌢 🌢🌢 🌢🌢🌢

○ Seed
○ Transplant

Plant Type
○ Vegetable   ○ Ornamental
○ Fruit   ○ Herb

Life Cycle: ○ Annual   ○ Biennial   ○ Perennial

SOWN FROM SEED	STARTED TRANSPLANT
Supplier:	Supplier:
Cost:	Cost:
Date Sown:	Date Planted:
Date Germinated:	Date Bloomed:
Date Planted Out:	**RATE IT:** ☆ ☆ ☆ ☆ ☆
Date Bloomed:	

Date	Event

Outcome	Uses

Notes

| Plant Name: | Purchased at: |
| Date Planted: | Price: |

Sunlight: ☼ ☀ ●

Water: 💧 💧💧 💧💧💧

○ Seed
○ Transplant

Plant Type
○ Vegetable   ○ Ornamental
○ Fruit   ○ Herb

Life Cycle: ○ Annual   ○ Biennial   ○ Perennial

SOWN FROM SEED	STARTED TRANSPLANT
Supplier:	Supplier:
Cost:	Cost:
Date Sown:	Date Planted:
Date Germinated:	Date Bloomed:
Date Planted Out:	**RATE IT:** ☆ ☆ ☆ ☆ ☆
Date Bloomed:	

Date	Event

Outcome	Uses

Notes

Plant Name:	Purchased at:
Date Planted:	Price:

Sunlight: ☼ ☼ ●

Water: 🌢 🌢🌢 🌢🌢🌢

○ Seed
○ Transplant

Plant Type
○ Vegetable   ○ Ornamental
○ Fruit   ○ Herb

Life Cycle: ○ Annual   ○ Biennial   ○ Perennial

SOWN FROM SEED	STARTED TRANSPLANT
Supplier:	Supplier:
Cost:	Cost:
Date Sown:	Date Planted:
Date Germinated:	Date Bloomed:
Date Planted Out:	**RATE IT:** ☆☆☆☆☆
Date Bloomed:	

Date	Event

Outcome	Uses

Notes

Plant Name:	Purchased at:
Date Planted:	Price:

Sunlight: ☼ ☼ ●

Water: 💧 💧💧 💧💧💧

○ Seed
○ Transplant

Plant Type
○ Vegetable   ○ Ornamental
○ Fruit   ○ Herb

Life Cycle: ○ Annual   ○ Biennial   ○ Perennial

SOWN FROM SEED	STARTED TRANSPLANT
Supplier:	Supplier:
Cost:	Cost:
Date Sown:	Date Planted:
Date Germinated:	Date Bloomed:
Date Planted Out:	**RATE IT:** ☆ ☆ ☆ ☆ ☆
Date Bloomed:	

Date	Event

Outcome	Uses

Notes

Plant Name:	Purchased at:
Date Planted:	Price:

Sunlight: ☼ ☼ ●

Water: 💧 💧💧 💧💧💧

◯ Seed

◯ Transplant

Plant Type

◯ Vegetable ◯ Ornamental

◯ Fruit ◯ Herb

Life Cycle: ◯ Annual ◯ Biennial ◯ Perennial

SOWN FROM SEED	STARTED TRANSPLANT
Supplier:	Supplier:
Cost:	Cost:
Date Sown:	Date Planted:
Date Germinated:	Date Bloomed:
Date Planted Out:	**RATE IT:** ☆ ☆ ☆ ☆ ☆
Date Bloomed:	

Date	Event

Outcome	Uses

Notes

Plant Name:	Purchased at:
Date Planted:	Price:

Sunlight: ☼ ☼ ●

Water: 🌢 🌢🌢 🌢🌢🌢

○ Seed
○ Transplant

Plant Type
○ Vegetable   ○ Ornamental
○ Fruit   ○ Herb

Life Cycle: ○ Annual   ○ Biennial   ○ Perennial

SOWN FROM SEED	STARTED TRANSPLANT
Supplier:	Supplier:
Cost:	Cost:
Date Sown:	Date Planted:
Date Germinated:	Date Bloomed:
Date Planted Out:	**RATE IT:** ☆ ☆ ☆ ☆ ☆
Date Bloomed:	

Date	Event

Outcome	Uses

Notes

Plant Name:	Purchased at:
Date Planted:	Price:

Sunlight: ☼ ☼ ●

Water: 💧 💧💧 💧💧💧

○ Seed
○ Transplant

Plant Type
○ Vegetable   ○ Ornamental
○ Fruit   ○ Herb

Life Cycle: ○ Annual   ○ Biennial   ○ Perennial

SOWN FROM SEED	STARTED TRANSPLANT
Supplier:	Supplier:
Cost:	Cost:
Date Sown:	Date Planted:
Date Germinated:	Date Bloomed:
Date Planted Out:	**RATE IT:** ☆ ☆ ☆ ☆ ☆
Date Bloomed:	

Date	Event

Outcome	Uses

Notes

Plant Name:	Purchased at:
Date Planted:	Price:

Sunlight: ☼ ☼ ●

Water: 💧 💧💧 💧💧💧

○ Seed
○ Transplant

Plant Type
○ Vegetable ○ Ornamental
○ Fruit ○ Herb

Life Cycle: ○ Annual ○ Biennial ○ Perennial

SOWN FROM SEED	STARTED TRANSPLANT
Supplier:	Supplier:
Cost:	Cost:
Date Sown:	Date Planted:
Date Germinated:	Date Bloomed:
Date Planted Out:	**RATE IT:** ☆ ☆ ☆ ☆ ☆
Date Bloomed:	

Date	Event

Outcome	Uses

Notes

Plant Name:	Purchased at:
Date Planted:	Price:

Sunlight: ☼ ☼ ●

Water: 🌢 🌢🌢 🌢🌢🌢

○ Seed
○ Transplant

Plant Type
○ Vegetable ○ Ornamental
○ Fruit ○ Herb

Life Cycle: ○ Annual ○ Biennial ○ Perennial

SOWN FROM SEED	STARTED TRANSPLANT
Supplier:	Supplier:
Cost:	Cost:
Date Sown:	Date Planted:
Date Germinated:	Date Bloomed:
Date Planted Out:	**RATE IT:** ☆☆☆☆☆
Date Bloomed:	

Date	Event

Outcome	Uses

Notes

Plant Name:	Purchased at:
Date Planted:	Price:

Sunlight: ☼ ☼ ●

Water: 💧 💧💧 💧💧💧

○ Seed
○ Transplant

Plant Type
○ Vegetable   ○ Ornamental
○ Fruit   ○ Herb

Life Cycle: ○ Annual   ○ Biennial   ○ Perennial

SOWN FROM SEED	STARTED TRANSPLANT
Supplier:	Supplier:
Cost:	Cost:
Date Sown:	Date Planted:
Date Germinated:	Date Bloomed:
Date Planted Out:	**RATE IT:** ☆ ☆ ☆ ☆ ☆
Date Bloomed:	

Date	Event

Outcome	Uses

Notes

Plant Name:	Purchased at:
Date Planted:	Price:

Sunlight: ☀ ☀ ●

Water: 💧 💧💧 💧💧💧

○ Seed
○ Transplant

Plant Type
○ Vegetable ○ Ornamental
○ Fruit ○ Herb

Life Cycle: ○ Annual ○ Biennial ○ Perennial

SOWN FROM SEED	STARTED TRANSPLANT
Supplier:	Supplier:
Cost:	Cost:
Date Sown:	Date Planted:
Date Germinated:	Date Bloomed:
Date Planted Out:	**RATE IT:** ☆ ☆ ☆ ☆ ☆
Date Bloomed:	

Date	Event

Outcome	Uses

Notes

| Plant Name: | Purchased at: |
| Date Planted: | Price: |

Sunlight: ☼ ☼ ●

Water: 💧 💧💧 💧💧💧

○ Seed
○ Transplant

Plant Type
○ Vegetable   ○ Ornamental
○ Fruit   ○ Herb

Life Cycle: ○ Annual   ○ Biennial   ○ Perennial

SOWN FROM SEED	STARTED TRANSPLANT
Supplier:	Supplier:
Cost:	Cost:
Date Sown:	Date Planted:
Date Germinated:	Date Bloomed:
Date Planted Out:	**RATE IT:** ☆ ☆ ☆ ☆ ☆
Date Bloomed:	

Date	Event

Outcome	Uses

Notes

Plant Name:	Purchased at:
Date Planted:	Price:

Sunlight: ☼ ☼ ●

Water: 💧 💧💧 💧💧💧

○ Seed
○ Transplant

Plant Type
○ Vegetable   ○ Ornamental
○ Fruit   ○ Herb

Life Cycle: ○ Annual   ○ Biennial   ○ Perennial

SOWN FROM SEED	STARTED TRANSPLANT
Supplier:	Supplier:
Cost:	Cost:
Date Sown	Date Planted:
Date Germinated:	Date Bloomed:
Date Planted Out	**RATE IT:** ☆☆☆☆☆
Date Bloomed:	

Date	Event

Outcome	**Uses**

Notes

| Plant Name: | Purchased at: |
| Date Planted: | Price: |

Sunlight: ☼ ☼ ●

Water: 🌢 🌢🌢 🌢🌢🌢

○ Seed
○ Transplant

Plant Type
○ Vegetable   ○ Ornamental
○ Fruit   ○ Herb

Life Cycle: ○ Annual   ○ Biennial   ○ Perennial

SOWN FROM SEED	STARTED TRANSPLANT
Supplier:	Supplier:
Cost:	Cost:
Date Sown:	Date Planted:
Date Germinated:	Date Bloomed:
Date Planted Out:	**RATE IT:** ☆☆☆☆☆
Date Bloomed:	

Date	Event

Outcome	Uses

Notes

Plant Name:	Purchased at:
Date Planted:	Price:

Sunlight: ☼ ☼ ●

Water: 🌢 🌢🌢 🌢🌢🌢

○ Seed
○ Transplant

Plant Type
○ Vegetable ○ Ornamental
○ Fruit ○ Herb

Life Cycle: ○ Annual ○ Biennial ○ Perennial

SOWN FROM SEED	STARTED TRANSPLANT
Supplier:	Supplier:
Cost:	Cost:
Date Sown:	Date Planted:
Date Germinated:	Date Bloomed:
Date Planted Out	**RATE IT:** ☆☆☆☆☆
Date Bloomed:	

Date	Event

Outcome	Uses

Notes

Plant Name:	Purchased at:
Date Planted:	Price:

Sunlight: ☼ ☼ ●

Water: 💧 💧💧 💧💧💧

○ Seed
○ Transplant

Plant Type
○ Vegetable ○ Ornamental
○ Fruit ○ Herb

Life Cycle: ○ Annual ○ Biennial ○ Perennial

SOWN FROM SEED	STARTED TRANSPLANT
Supplier:	Supplier:
Cost:	Cost:
Date Sown:	Date Planted:
Date Germinated:	Date Bloomed:
Date Planted Out:	**RATE IT:** ☆ ☆ ☆ ☆ ☆
Date Bloomed:	

Date	Event

Outcome	Uses

Notes

Plant Name:	Purchased at:
Date Planted:	Price:

Sunlight: ☼ ☼ ●

Water: 💧 💧💧 💧💧💧

○ Seed

○ Transplant

Plant Type

○ Vegetable ○ Ornamental
○ Fruit ○ Herb

Life Cycle: ○ Annual ○ Biennial ○ Perennial

SOWN FROM SEED	STARTED TRANSPLANT
Supplier:	Supplier:
Cost:	Cost:
Date Sown:	Date Planted:
Date Germinated:	Date Bloomed:
Date Planted Out:	**RATE IT:** ☆ ☆ ☆ ☆ ☆
Date Bloomed:	

Date	Event

Outcome	Uses

Notes

Plant Name:	Purchased at:
Date Planted:	Price:

Sunlight: ☼ ☼ ●

Water: 💧 💧💧 💧💧💧

○ Seed

○ Transplant

Plant Type

○ Vegetable ○ Ornamental
○ Fruit ○ Herb

Life Cycle: ○ Annual ○ Biennial ○ Perennial

SOWN FROM SEED	STARTED TRANSPLANT
Supplier:	Supplier:
Cost:	Cost:
Date Sown:	Date Planted:
Date Germinated:	Date Bloomed:
Date Planted Out	**RATE IT:** ☆ ☆ ☆ ☆ ☆
Date Bloomed:	

Date	Event

Outcome	Uses

Notes

Plant Name:	Purchased at:
Date Planted:	Price:

Sunlight: ☼ ☼ ●

Water: 💧 💧💧 💧💧💧

○ Seed
○ Transplant

Plant Type
○ Vegetable ○ Ornamental
○ Fruit ○ Herb

Life Cycle: ○ Annual ○ Biennial ○ Perennial

SOWN FROM SEED	STARTED TRANSPLANT
Supplier:	Supplier:
Cost:	Cost:
Date Sown	Date Planted:
Date Germinated:	Date Bloomed:
Date Planted Out	**RATE IT:** ☆ ☆ ☆ ☆ ☆
Date Bloomed:	

Date	Event

Outcome	Uses

Notes

Plant Name:	Purchased at:
Date Planted:	Price:

Sunlight: ☼ ☼ ●

Water: 💧 💧💧 💧💧💧

○ Seed
○ Transplant

Plant Type
○ Vegetable   ○ Ornamental
○ Fruit   ○ Herb

Life Cycle: ○ Annual   ○ Biennial   ○ Perennial

SOWN FROM SEED	STARTED TRANSPLANT
Supplier:	Supplier:
Cost:	Cost:
Date Sown:	Date Planted:
Date Germinated:	Date Bloomed:
Date Planted Out:	**RATE IT:** ☆ ☆ ☆ ☆ ☆
Date Bloomed:	

Date	Event

Outcome	Uses

Notes

Plant Name:	Purchased at:
Date Planted:	Price:

Sunlight: ☼ ☼ ●

Water: 💧 💧💧 💧💧💧

○ Seed
○ Transplant

Plant Type
○ Vegetable ○ Ornamental
○ Fruit ○ Herb

Life Cycle: ○ Annual ○ Biennial ○ Perennial

SOWN FROM SEED	STARTED TRANSPLANT
Supplier:	Supplier:
Cost:	Cost:
Date Sown:	Date Planted:
Date Germinated:	Date Bloomed:
Date Planted Out:	**RATE IT:** ☆☆☆☆☆
Date Bloomed:	

Date	Event

Outcome	Uses

Notes

| Plant Name: | Purchased at: |
| Date Planted: | Price: |

Sunlight: ☼ ☼ ●

Water: 🌢 🌢🌢 🌢🌢🌢

○ Seed
○ Transplant

Plant Type
○ Vegetable   ○ Ornamental
○ Fruit   ○ Herb

Life Cycle: ○ Annual   ○ Biennial   ○ Perennial

SOWN FROM SEED	STARTED TRANSPLANT
Supplier:	Supplier:
Cost:	Cost:
Date Sown:	Date Planted:
Date Germinated:	Date Bloomed:
Date Planted Out:	**RATE IT:** ☆☆☆☆☆
Date Bloomed:	

Date	Event

Outcome	Uses

Notes

Plant Name:	Purchased at:
Date Planted:	Price:

Sunlight: ☼ ☼ ●

Water: 🌢 🌢🌢 🌢🌢🌢

○ Seed

○ Transplant

Plant Type
○ Vegetable   ○ Ornamental
○ Fruit   ○ Herb

Life Cycle: ○ Annual   ○ Biennial   ○ Perennial

SOWN FROM SEED	STARTED TRANSPLANT
Supplier:	Supplier:
Cost:	Cost:
Date Sown:	Date Planted:
Date Germinated:	Date Bloomed:
Date Planted Out:	**RATE IT:** ☆☆☆☆☆
Date Bloomed:	

Date	Event

Outcome	Uses

Notes

| Plant Name: | Purchased at: |
| Date Planted: | Price: |

Sunlight: ☀ ☀ ●

Water: 💧 💧💧 💧💧💧

◯ Seed
◯ Transplant

Plant Type
◯ Vegetable ◯ Ornamental
◯ Fruit ◯ Herb

Life Cycle: ◯ Annual ◯ Biennial ◯ Perennial

SOWN FROM SEED	STARTED TRANSPLANT
Supplier:	Supplier:
Cost:	Cost:
Date Sown:	Date Planted:
Date Germinated:	Date Bloomed:
Date Planted Out:	**RATE IT:** ☆ ☆ ☆ ☆ ☆
Date Bloomed:	

Date	Event

Outcome	Uses

Notes

Plant Name:	Purchased at:
Date Planted:	Price:

Sunlight: ☼ ☼ ●

Water: 💧 💧💧 💧💧💧

○ Seed
○ Transplant

Plant Type
○ Vegetable   ○ Ornamental
○ Fruit   ○ Herb

Life Cycle: ○ Annual   ○ Biennial   ○ Perennial

SOWN FROM SEED	STARTED TRANSPLANT
Supplier:	Supplier:
Cost:	Cost:
Date Sown:	Date Planted:
Date Germinated:	Date Bloomed:
Date Planted Out:	**RATE IT:** ☆ ☆ ☆ ☆ ☆
Date Bloomed:	

Date	Event

Outcome	Uses

Notes

| Plant Name: | Purchased at: |
| Date Planted: | Price: |

Sunlight: ☼ ☼ ⬤　　○ Seed

Water: 🌢 🌢🌢 🌢🌢🌢　　○ Transplant

Plant Type
○ Vegetable　　○ Ornamental
○ Fruit　　○ Herb

Life Cycle: ○ Annual　　○ Biennial　　○ Perennial

SOWN FROM SEED	STARTED TRANSPLANT
Supplier:	Supplier:
Cost:	Cost:
Date Sown:	Date Planted:
Date Germinated:	Date Bloomed:
Date Planted Out:	**RATE IT:** ☆ ☆ ☆ ☆ ☆
Date Bloomed:	

Date	Event

Outcome	Uses

Notes

Plant Name:	Purchased at:
Date Planted:	Price:

Sunlight: ☼ ☼ ●

Water: 💧 💧💧 💧💧💧

○ Seed
○ Transplant

Plant Type
○ Vegetable ○ Ornamental
○ Fruit ○ Herb

Life Cycle: ○ Annual ○ Biennial ○ Perennial

SOWN FROM SEED	STARTED TRANSPLANT
Supplier:	Supplier:
Cost:	Cost:
Date Sown:	Date Planted:
Date Germinated:	Date Bloomed:
Date Planted Out:	**RATE IT:** ☆ ☆ ☆ ☆ ☆
Date Bloomed:	

Date	Event

Outcome	Uses

Notes

Plant Name:	Purchased at:
Date Planted:	Price:

Sunlight: ☀ ☀ ●

Water: 💧 💧💧 💧💧💧

○ Seed
○ Transplant

Plant Type
○ Vegetable   ○ Ornamental
○ Fruit   ○ Herb

Life Cycle: ○ Annual   ○ Biennial   ○ Perennial

SOWN FROM SEED	STARTED TRANSPLANT
Supplier:	Supplier:
Cost:	Cost:
Date Sown:	Date Planted:
Date Germinated:	Date Bloomed:
Date Planted Out:	**RATE IT:** ☆ ☆ ☆ ☆ ☆
Date Bloomed:	

Date	Event

Outcome	Uses

Notes

Plant Name:	Purchased at:
Date Planted:	Price:

Sunlight: ☼ ☼ ●

Water: 💧 💧💧 💧💧💧

○ Seed

○ Transplant

Plant Type
○ Vegetable ○ Ornamental
○ Fruit ○ Herb

Life Cycle: ○ Annual ○ Biennial ○ Perennial

SOWN FROM SEED	STARTED TRANSPLANT
Supplier:	Supplier:
Cost:	Cost:
Date Sown:	Date Planted:
Date Germinated:	Date Bloomed:
Date Planted Out:	**RATE IT:** ☆ ☆ ☆ ☆ ☆
Date Bloomed:	

Date	Event

Outcome	Uses

Notes

Plant Name:	Purchased at:
Date Planted:	Price:

Sunlight: ☼ ☼ ●

Water: 🌢 🌢🌢 🌢🌢🌢

○ Seed
○ Transplant

Plant Type
○ Vegetable ○ Ornamental
○ Fruit ○ Herb

Life Cycle: ○ Annual ○ Biennial ○ Perennial

SOWN FROM SEED	STARTED TRANSPLANT
Supplier:	Supplier:
Cost:	Cost:
Date Sown:	Date Planted:
Date Germinated:	Date Bloomed:
Date Planted Out:	**RATE IT:** ☆☆☆☆☆
Date Bloomed:	

Date	Event

Outcome	Uses

Notes

Plant Name:	Purchased at:
Date Planted:	Price:

Sunlight: ☼ ☼ ●

Water: 💧 💧💧 💧💧💧

○ Seed
○ Transplant

Plant Type
○ Vegetable   ○ Ornamental
○ Fruit   ○ Herb

Life Cycle: ○ Annual   ○ Biennial   ○ Perennial

SOWN FROM SEED	STARTED TRANSPLANT
Supplier:	Supplier:
Cost:	Cost:
Date Sown:	Date Planted:
Date Germinated:	Date Bloomed:
Date Planted Out:	**RATE IT:** ☆ ☆ ☆ ☆ ☆
Date Bloomed:	

Date	Event

Outcome	Uses

Notes

Plant Name:	Purchased at:
Date Planted:	Price:

Sunlight: ☼ ☼ ●

Water: 💧 💧💧 💧💧💧

○ Seed
○ Transplant

Plant Type
○ Vegetable ○ Ornamental
○ Fruit ○ Herb

Life Cycle: ○ Annual ○ Biennial ○ Perennial

SOWN FROM SEED	STARTED TRANSPLANT
Supplier:	Supplier:
Cost:	Cost:
Date Sown:	Date Planted:
Date Germinated:	Date Bloomed:
Date Planted Out:	**RATE IT:** ☆ ☆ ☆ ☆ ☆
Date Bloomed:	

Date	Event

Outcome	Uses

Notes

Plant Name:	Purchased at:
Date Planted:	Price:

Sunlight: ☼ ☼ ●

Water: 💧 💧💧 💧💧💧

○ Seed
○ Transplant

Plant Type
○ Vegetable ○ Ornamental
○ Fruit ○ Herb

Life Cycle: ○ Annual ○ Biennial ○ Perennial

SOWN FROM SEED	STARTED TRANSPLANT
Supplier:	Supplier:
Cost:	Cost:
Date Sown:	Date Planted:
Date Germinated:	Date Bloomed:
Date Planted Out:	**RATE IT:** ☆ ☆ ☆ ☆ ☆
Date Bloomed:	

Date	Event

Outcome	Uses

Notes

Plant Name:	Purchased at:
Date Planted:	Price:

Sunlight: ☼ ☼ ●

Water: 🌢 🌢🌢 🌢🌢🌢

○ Seed

○ Transplant

Plant Type

○ Vegetable   ○ Ornamental
○ Fruit   ○ Herb

Life Cycle: ○ Annual   ○ Biennial   ○ Perennial

SOWN FROM SEED	STARTED TRANSPLANT
Supplier:	Supplier:
Cost:	Cost:
Date Sown:	Date Planted:
Date Germinated:	Date Bloomed:
Date Planted Out:	**RATE IT:** ☆☆☆☆☆
Date Bloomed:	

Date	Event

Outcome	Uses

Notes

| Plant Name: | Purchased at: |
| Date Planted: | Price: |

Sunlight: ☀ ☀ ●

Water: 💧 💧💧 💧💧💧

○ Seed
○ Transplant

Plant Type
○ Vegetable   ○ Ornamental
○ Fruit   ○ Herb

Life Cycle: ○ Annual   ○ Biennial   ○ Perennial

SOWN FROM SEED	STARTED TRANSPLANT
Supplier:	Supplier:
Cost:	Cost:
Date Sown:	Date Planted:
Date Germinated:	Date Bloomed:
Date Planted Out:	**RATE IT:** ☆ ☆ ☆ ☆ ☆
Date Bloomed:	

Date	Event

Outcome	**Uses**

Notes

| Plant Name: | Purchased at: |
| Date Planted: | Price: |

Sunlight: ☼ ☼ ●

Water: 🌢 🌢🌢 🌢🌢🌢

○ Seed
○ Transplant

Plant Type
○ Vegetable   ○ Ornamental
○ Fruit   ○ Herb

Life Cycle: ○ Annual   ○ Biennial   ○ Perennial

SOWN FROM SEED	STARTED TRANSPLANT
Supplier:	Supplier:
Cost:	Cost:
Date Sown:	Date Planted:
Date Germinated:	Date Bloomed:
Date Planted Out	**RATE IT:** ☆ ☆ ☆ ☆ ☆
Date Bloomed:	

Date	Event

Outcome	**Uses**

Notes

Plant Name:	Purchased at:
Date Planted:	Price:

Sunlight: ☼ ☼ ●

Water: 💧 💧💧 💧💧💧

○ Seed

○ Transplant

Plant Type
○ Vegetable ○ Ornamental
○ Fruit ○ Herb

Life Cycle: ○ Annual ○ Biennial ○ Perennial

SOWN FROM SEED	STARTED TRANSPLANT
Supplier:	Supplier:
Cost:	Cost:
Date Sown:	Date Planted:
Date Germinated:	Date Bloomed:
Date Planted Out:	**RATE IT:** ☆ ☆ ☆ ☆ ☆
Date Bloomed:	

Date	Event

Outcome	Uses

Notes

Plant Name:	Purchased at:
Date Planted:	Price:

Sunlight: ☼ ☼ ●

Water: 💧 💧💧 💧💧💧

○ Seed
○ Transplant

Plant Type
○ Vegetable   ○ Ornamental
○ Fruit   ○ Herb

Life Cycle: ○ Annual   ○ Biennial   ○ Perennial

SOWN FROM SEED	STARTED TRANSPLANT
Supplier:	Supplier:
Cost:	Cost:
Date Sown:	Date Planted:
Date Germinated:	Date Bloomed:
Date Planted Out:	**RATE IT:** ☆ ☆ ☆ ☆ ☆
Date Bloomed:	

Date	Event

Outcome	Uses

Notes

Plant Name:	Purchased at:
Date Planted:	Price:

Sunlight: ☼ ☼ ●

Water: 🌢 🌢🌢 🌢🌢🌢

◯ Seed
◯ Transplant

Plant Type
◯ Vegetable ◯ Ornamental
◯ Fruit ◯ Herb

Life Cycle: ◯ Annual ◯ Biennial ◯ Perennial

SOWN FROM SEED	STARTED TRANSPLANT
Supplier:	Supplier:
Cost:	Cost:
Date Sown:	Date Planted:
Date Germinated:	Date Bloomed:
Date Planted Out:	**RATE IT:** ☆☆☆☆☆
Date Bloomed:	

Date	Event

Outcome	Uses

Notes

| Plant Name: | Purchased at: |
| Date Planted: | Price: |

Sunlight: ☀ ☼ ●

Water: 💧 💧💧 💧💧💧

○ Seed
○ Transplant

Plant Type
○ Vegetable   ○ Ornamental
○ Fruit   ○ Herb

Life Cycle: ○ Annual   ○ Biennial   ○ Perennial

SOWN FROM SEED	STARTED TRANSPLANT
Supplier:	Supplier:
Cost:	Cost:
Date Sown:	Date Planted:
Date Germinated:	Date Bloomed:
Date Planted Out:	**RATE IT:** ☆☆☆☆☆
Date Bloomed:	

Date	Event

Outcome	Uses

Notes

Plant Name:	Purchased at:
Date Planted:	Price:

Sunlight: ☼ ☼ ●

Water: ◗ ◗◗ ◗◗◗

○ Seed
○ Transplant

Plant Type
○ Vegetable   ○ Ornamental
○ Fruit   ○ Herb

Life Cycle: ○ Annual   ○ Biennial   ○ Perennial

SOWN FROM SEED	STARTED TRANSPLANT
Supplier:	Supplier:
Cost:	Cost:
Date Sown:	Date Planted:
Date Germinated:	Date Bloomed:
Date Planted Out:	**RATE IT:** ☆ ☆ ☆ ☆ ☆
Date Bloomed:	

Date	Event

Outcome	Uses

Notes

Plant Name:	Purchased at:
Date Planted:	Price:

Sunlight: ☼ ☼ ●

Water: 🌢 🌢🌢 🌢🌢🌢

○ Seed
○ Transplant

Plant Type
○ Vegetable   ○ Ornamental
○ Fruit   ○ Herb

Life Cycle: ○ Annual   ○ Biennial   ○ Perennial

SOWN FROM SEED	STARTED TRANSPLANT
Supplier:	Supplier:
Cost:	Cost:
Date Sown:	Date Planted:
Date Germinated:	Date Bloomed:
Date Planted Out:	**RATE IT:** ☆☆☆☆☆
Date Bloomed:	

Date	Event

Outcome	Uses

Notes

Plant Name:	Purchased at:
Date Planted:	Price:

Sunlight: ☀ ⛅ ●

Water: 🌢 🌢🌢 🌢🌢🌢

○ Seed

○ Transplant

Plant Type

○ Vegetable ○ Ornamental
○ Fruit ○ Herb

Life Cycle: ○ Annual   ○ Biennial   ○ Perennial

SOWN FROM SEED	STARTED TRANSPLANT
Supplier:	Supplier:
Cost:	Cost:
Date Sown:	Date Planted:
Date Germinated:	Date Bloomed:
Date Planted Out	
Date Bloomed:	**RATE IT:** ☆ ☆ ☆ ☆ ☆

Date	Event

Outcome	Uses

Notes

Plant Name:	Purchased at:
Date Planted:	Price:

Sunlight: ☼ ☼ ●

Water: 🌢 🌢🌢 🌢🌢🌢

○ Seed
○ Transplant

Plant Type
○ Vegetable ○ Ornamental
○ Fruit ○ Herb

Life Cycle: ○ Annual ○ Biennial ○ Perennial

SOWN FROM SEED	STARTED TRANSPLANT
Supplier:	Supplier:
Cost:	Cost:
Date Sown:	Date Planted:
Date Germinated:	Date Bloomed:
Date Planted Out:	**RATE IT:** ☆☆☆☆☆
Date Bloomed:	

Date	Event

Outcome	Uses

Notes

Plant Name:	Purchased at:
Date Planted:	Price:

Sunlight: ☀ ☀ ●

Water: 🌢 🌢🌢 🌢🌢🌢

○ Seed
○ Transplant

Plant Type
○ Vegetable ○ Ornamental
○ Fruit ○ Herb

Life Cycle: ○ Annual ○ Biennial ○ Perennial

SOWN FROM SEED	STARTED TRANSPLANT
Supplier:	Supplier:
Cost:	Cost:
Date Sown:	Date Planted:
Date Germinated:	Date Bloomed:
Date Planted Out:	**RATE IT:** ☆ ☆ ☆ ☆ ☆
Date Bloomed:	

Date	Event

Outcome	Uses

Notes

Plant Name:	Purchased at:
Date Planted:	Price:

Sunlight: ☼ ☼ ●

Water: 💧 💧💧 💧💧💧

○ Seed
○ Transplant

Plant Type
○ Vegetable   ○ Ornamental
○ Fruit   ○ Herb

Life Cycle: ○ Annual   ○ Biennial   ○ Perennial

SOWN FROM SEED	STARTED TRANSPLANT
Supplier:	Supplier:
Cost:	Cost:
Date Sown:	Date Planted:
Date Germinated:	Date Bloomed:
Date Planted Out	**RATE IT:** ☆☆☆☆☆
Date Bloomed:	

Date	Event

Outcome	Uses

Notes

Plant Name:	Purchased at:
Date Planted:	Price:

Sunlight: ☼ ☼ ●

Water: 🌢 🌢🌢 🌢🌢🌢

◯ Seed

◯ Transplant

Plant Type
◯ Vegetable ◯ Ornamental
◯ Fruit ◯ Herb

Life Cycle: ◯ Annual ◯ Biennial ◯ Perennial

SOWN FROM SEED	STARTED TRANSPLANT
Supplier:	Supplier:
Cost:	Cost:
Date Sown:	Date Planted:
Date Germinated:	Date Bloomed:
Date Planted Out:	**RATE IT:** ☆ ☆ ☆ ☆ ☆
Date Bloomed:	

Date	Event

Outcome	Uses

Notes

Made in the USA
Coppell, TX
26 April 2024

31759049R00085